AF454328

ART COLLECTOR'S CHOICE

MIDDLE EAST

VOL. II

Published by
Contemporary Art Station

The Art Collector's Choice book is committed for Middle East and international art collectors,
curators, gallery owners and art enthusiasts, containing a curated selection
of the most investable artworks that will inspire art collectors around the globe.

كتاب اختيار الفن يتعد للفنانين، وأمناء المكتبات، وأصحاب المعارض، وعشاق
الفن من الشرق الأوسط وجميع أنحاء العالم، يتضمن مجموعة مختارة من
الأعمال الفنية الأكثر استثماراً والتي تلهم جامعي الفن في جميع أنحاء العالم

First published in Europe in April 2021 by the
Contemporary Art Station/ICM Gestora Cultural, SL.
All artworks @ 2021 the individual artists.
Measurements and title of artworks are supplied by
the artists.

ISBN: 978-84-18287-92-3
Author: Contemporay Art Station
Title: Art Collector 's Choice, Middle East. Volume II
D. L.: GR 496-2021
2021 © ICM Gestora Cultural, SL

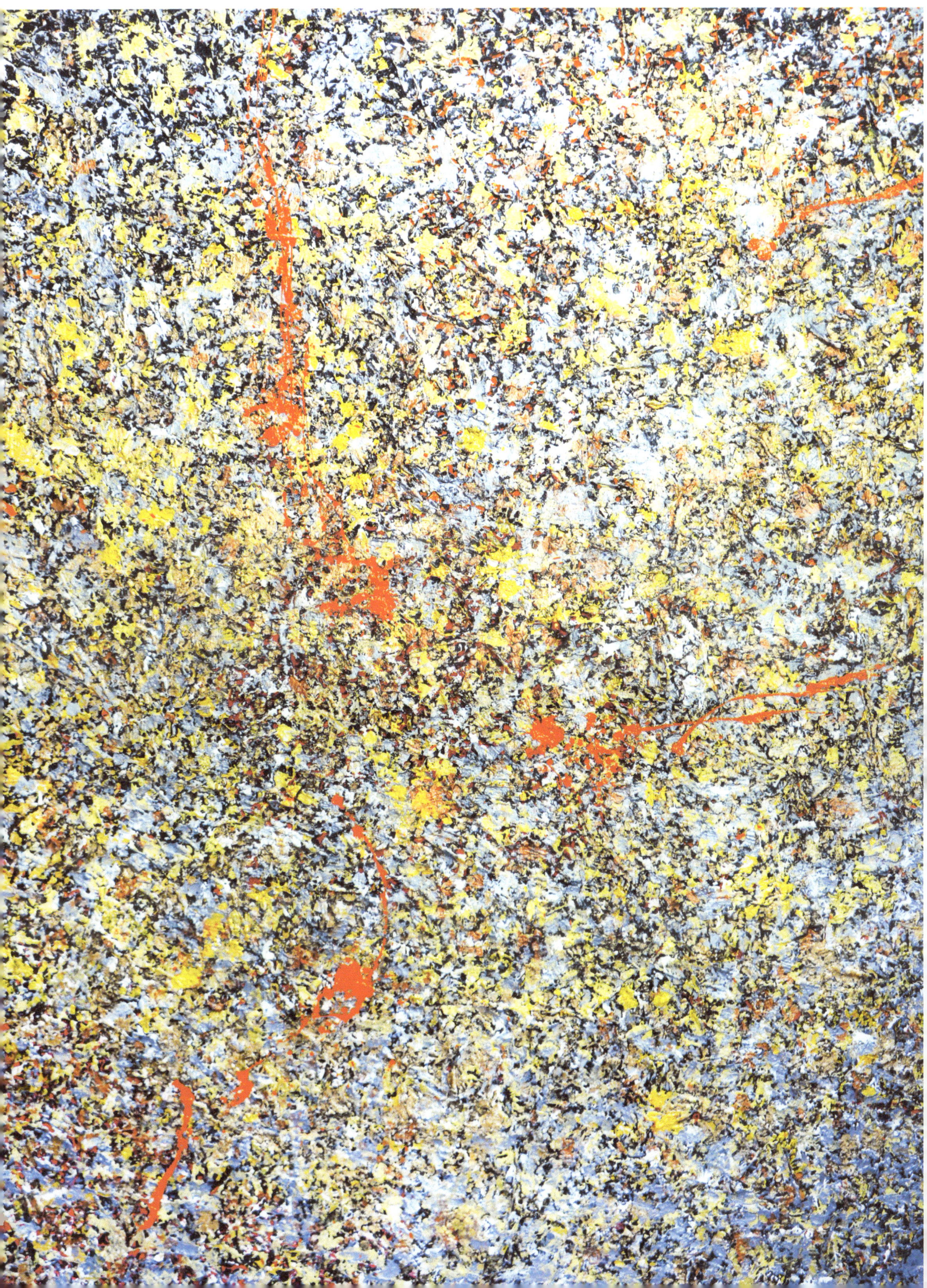

AMALIA BORIN
ANDRÉ SCHOOTS
ANGELIKA PRAPA
ANNE FELICIE NICKELS
ANNEMARIE AMBROSOLI
AOMI KIKUCHI
AUGUST VILELLA
BELLE ROTH
BARBARA KRAJEWSKA
BERTA JAYO
BO SONG
BRIGITTA WESTPHAL
CARLOS ARANHA
CAROLIN RECHBERG
CASPAR BAUM
CENGIZ YATAGAN
DANNY JOHANANOFF
DAVID TURNER FRSA
DUYGU KIVANC
ERIC HUBBES
ERIN STARR
FRANK MANN

HOWARD HARRIS
HÉLÈNE JACUBOWITZ
JAIME JOSÉ
JIAN KWON
JASMINE SEO
JOEY CRUZ MARGAREJO
JOHANNES EHEMANN
JORDI PIERA
KASPER DE GOUW
KAT KLEINMAN
KENCH WEATHERS
MARCO BENEDETTI
MARIA LINARES FREIRE
MAX WERNER
MICHAL ASHKENASI
PETRA SCHOTT
RONNIE JIANG
SOMSAK CHAITUCH
TJEERD DOOSJE
TOM RUPNICKI
URSA SCHOEPPER
YAROSLAVA LISEEVA

تم النشر بواسطة

**Contemporary
Art Station**

Ronnie Jiang

France | فرنسا

Ronnie Jiang was a fashion designer who launched her artistic career in 2013 in France. In 2019 she started to work on a series that she called Déstructuralisme Figurative, she focuses on the evolution of the "form", the destructuring of bodies and faces in which joyful anatomy is built and deconstructed in the footsteps of cubism. The geometrized but still realistic fleshly fragments identify without flaws and are released in their contortions. In Ronnie's work, we can detect a few characters from cartoons mixed with faces or body parts. These new disfigured, strange, and imposing creatures show a certain spatiality of forms. Their juxtapositions induce the possibility of a new story. Ronnie is deconstructing to reconstruct to discover a new form and new story.

روني جيانج كانت مصممة أزياء بدأت مسيرتها المهنية عام 2013 في فرنسا. في عام 2019 بدأت العمل على سلسلة سمتها ديستراكتوراليزم فيجوراتيف، ركزت فيها على ثورة "التشكيل"، التحطيم في الأجساد والوجوه بحيث يتم بناء وتفكيك التشريح الممتع على خطى التكعيب الهندسي. تشكيل هندسي مع كونه مكون من قطع جسدية واقعية تحدد بدون عيوب ويتم اطلاقها في التواءاتها. في عمل روني، نستطيع أن نكتشف بعض الشخصيات من الرسوم المتحركة مدمجة مع وجوه أو أعضاء جسدية. هذه المخلوقات المشوهة، والغريبة، والمهيبة تظهر مكانية مؤكدة في الأشكال. تجانبها يستحدث احتمالية قصة جديدة. روني تحطم لتعيد البناء لتكتشف شكلاً جديداً وقصة جديدة.

Grrr..., 80 cm x 80 cm, Acrylic on canvas, 2019

Forward Backward, 80 cm x 80 cm, Acrylic on canvas, 2019

Ronnie Jiang

Untitled #2, 50 cm x 50 cm, Acrylic on canvas, 2020

Untitled #3, 50 cm x 50 cm, Acrylic on canvas, 2020

August Vilella

August Vilella is an artist based in Tokyo. His works have been exhibited around the world and he was awarded in Tokyo, Dubai and twice in Taiwan for his art. He creates oil paintings by means of a surreal-intuitive method. Thanks to this process, he tries to give shape to his subconscious mind without using any previous sketches or ideas. The result of this practice evokes a dreamlike aura and metaphorical and philosophical language, which invites the audience to reflect. All this iconography is represented with a very refined technic. In consequence, we can see in Vilella´s artworks a very curious contrast between a very technical and elaborated style, and a creative process that turns out to be completely intuitively improvised and unintentional …

أوجست فيليلا هو فنان مقيم في طوكيو. تعرض أعماله في جميع أنحاء العالم وتم تكريمه في طوكيو، ودبي ومرتين في تايوان لفنه. يصنع لوحات زيتية بطريقة سريالية بديهية. الشكر الجزيل لطريقته، إنه يحاول اعطاء الأشكال لعقله الباطن بدون استخدام رسوماته أو أفكاره السابقة. نتيجة هذه الممارسة يستحضرهالة تشبه الحلم ولغة مجازية وفلسفية، والتي تدعو الجمهور للتفكير. جميع هذه الأيقونية يتم تقديمها بتقنية متناهية الدقة. بالتالي، نستطيع أن نرى في أعمال فيليلا الفنية تبايناً فضولياً جداً بين النمط التقني والمفصل، و الطريقة الإبداعية التي تتحول لتصبح مرتجلة بشكل حدسي تمامًا وغير مقصودة ...

Bee

Sailor´s Look

August Vilella

Hope

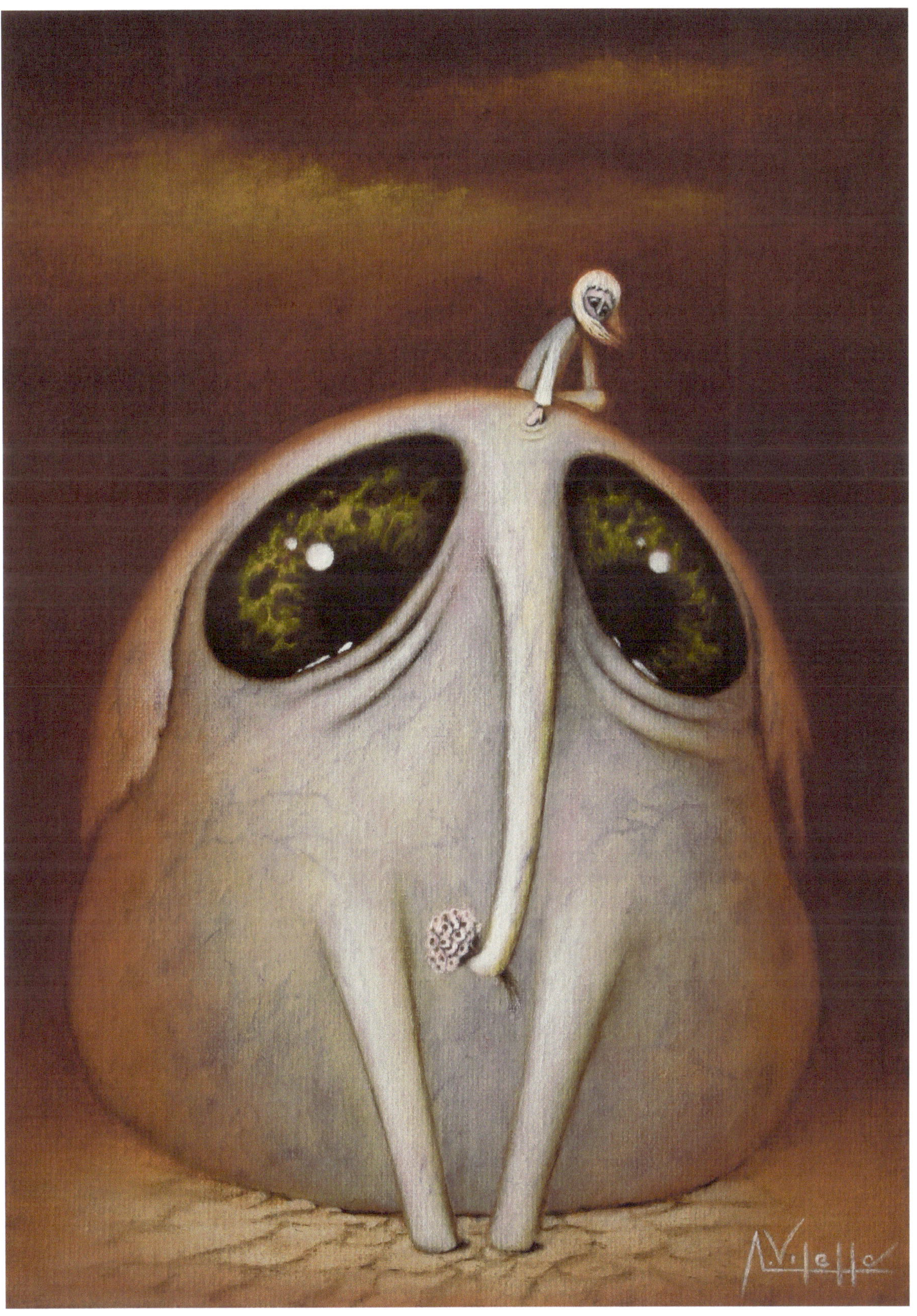

Sailor´s Look

David Turner FRSA

David Turner FRSA is a well known visual artist whose work has been shown in galleries and public spaces on three continents. Upcoming exhibitions of his work include displays in London, Hong Kong, Tokyo, and Barcelona. He is also a poet and a playwright/screenwriter and is currently writing a book on Sir Joshua Reynolds. He is a Fellow of the Royal Society of Arts (RSA) a London based "creative think tank" founded in 1754.

ديفيد تيرنر فرسا هو فنان تشكيلي معروف والذي أعماله تم عرضها في صالات عرض وساحات عامة في ثلاثة قارات. المعارض القادمة لأعماله تشمل شاشات في لندن، وهونج كونج، ولندن، وطوكيو، وبرشلونا. وهو أيضًا شاعر وكاتب مسرحي / كاتب سيناريو ويقوم حالياً بكتابة كتاب عن السيد جوشوا رينولدز. وهو زميل الجمعية الملكية للفنون (أر أس اي) والتي مقرها في لندن "خزان التفكير الإبداعي" أسست عام 1754.

In Medici Res, Fine Art Print, 2019

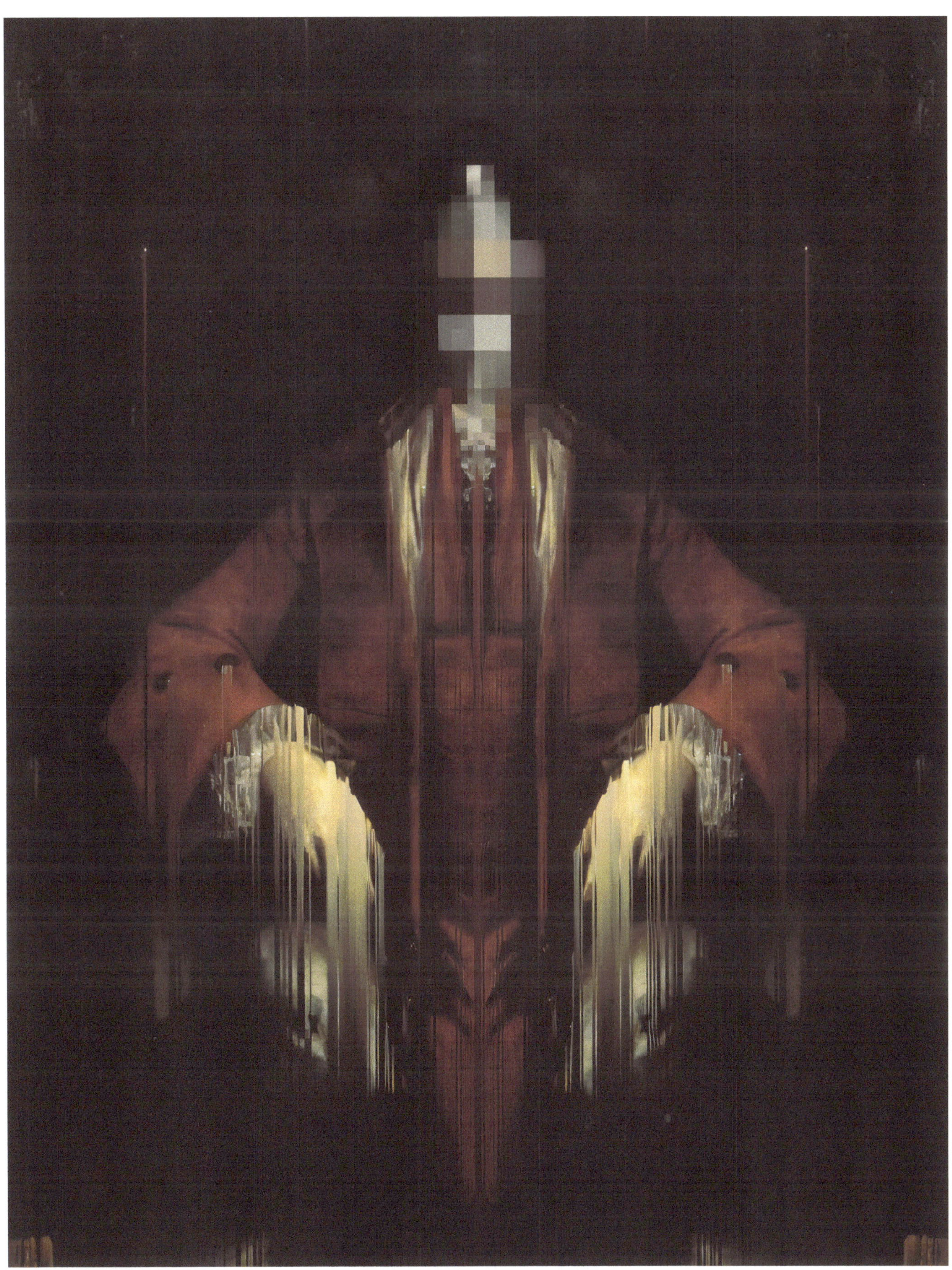

American Gothic - Fine Art Print (2021)

Never Follow A Hippie To A Second Location - Fine Art Print (2021)

After Tara - Fine Art Print (2021)

Carlos Aranha

Internacional Art Award Winner, Canadian/Ecuadorian, Painter, Sculptor, Art Installer and a Documentary Producer. Aranha' artwork can be found in permanent collections in Museums such as: Fantapia Museum, South Korea - Haegeumgan Theme Museum, South Korea - Ministry of Culture, National Cultural Center, Cairo Opera House, Cairo Egypt - YukYung Art Museum, South Korea - Dominican Man Museum, Dominican Republic - Museum Casa de la Cultura Ecuatoriana, Ecuador- Museo Confamiliar, Colombia, amongst others. My artwork is like an exploration, a "Circle of Life" that swirls and meanders falling eventually into its own rhythm. I use acrylics and recycled materials to create my artwork, my goal is to convey messages of hope as well as respect for nature and the environment.

حائز على جوائز فن عالمية، كندي/اكوادري، رسام، نحات، صانع فن، ومنتج أفلام وثائقية. الأعمال الفنية "أرنها" يمكن ايجادها في مجموعات دائمة في المتاجف مثل: متحف فانتابيا، كوريا الجنوبية – متحف هيجيمجان الفني، كوريا الجنوبية – وزارة الثقافة، المركز الثقافي الوطني،دار الأوبرا في القاهرة، القاهرة مصر – متحف يوكيانج للفن، كوريا الجنوبية – متحف الرجل الدومينيكي، جمهورية الدومينيك – متحف كاسا دي لا كالتشارا ايكواتوريانا، الاكوادور – ميوزيو كونفاميليار، كولومبيا، من بين أماكن أخرى. أعمالي الفنية تشبه الاستكشاف، مثل "دوامة الحياة" التي تدور وتتعرج وتهبط في نهاية المطاف على إيقاعها الخاص. أستخدم الأكريليك والمواد المعاد تدويرها لصنع أعمالي الفنية، هدفي هو ايصال رسائل من الأمل بالإضافة إلى الاحترام والإجلال للطبيعة والبيئة.

Title: " Spring " Technique: Acrylic on Canvas Size: 152 Cm x 152 Cm Year: 2020

Title: " Autumn " Technique: Acrylic on Canvas Size: 152 Cm x 152 Cm. Year: 2020

Carlos Aranha

Title: "Red Moon" Technique: Acrylic on Canvas Size: 92 Cm x 107 Cm. Year: 2020

Title: "Stay" Technique: Acrylic on Canvas Size: 92 Cm x 107 Cm. Year : 2020

Tom Rupnicki

NightOrbs™ magically transforms outdoor space with the beauty and glow of hand-blown glass. These distinctive illuminators blend function and artistry to create enchanting lighting for landscape or water features, and serve as distinctive garden accents. Each hand-blown glass orb is an original work of durable art that comes with its own two-part sealed cast-aluminum bronze powder-coated base, or upgrade to a cast silicon bronze base. NightOrb are low-voltage lighting (12 volts) and use a long-life, 20-watt up to 50 watt LED lamp that provides ambient light for illumination of areas up to 100 square feet. They come in 4", 8", 13", & 18" in diameter.

"نايت أوربس" حولت بشكل سحري الفضاء الخارجي إلى نافخ يدوي زجاجي في منتهى الجمال والتوهج. تمزج هذه الأضواء المميزة الوظيفة بالفن لتخلق اضاءة رائعة للمناظر الطبيعية والنوافير المائية، وتخدم كعناصر مهمة في الحديقة بشكل مميز. كل من هذه النافخات الزجاجية اليدوية تشكل عملاً فنياً أصيلاً وتكون مزودة بقاعدة مصنوعة من الالمنيوم الخالص ومطلية باللون البرونزي، أو متطورة عن ذلك بأن تكون مصنوعة من السيليكون الخالص بلون برونزي. نايت أورب عبارة عن ضوء منخفض الجهد (12 فولت) مزودة بمصباح ليد طويل الأمد (20 واط يصل إلى 50 واط) وتستطيع إضاءة ساحة بمسطح تصل إلى 100 قدم مربع. متعددة القياسات بقطر 4، 8، 13، 18 بوصة.

Swimming pool surronded by 14 NightOrbs 13" & 8"

Four White 18 inch NightOrbs along garden path.

Tom Rupnicki

Assortment of 13 inch and 8 inch NightOrbs ascending granite steps

18" Sun NightOrb in Philadelphia Flower show exhibit Best in show.

Petra Schott

I was born in Germany in 1953, studied fine arts in Kassel/ Germany and started taking part in exhibitions nationally and internationally as of 1993. I am part of the national association of professional artists (BBK) and of the national association of professional female artists (GEDOK). My most recent catalogue "Into the open" is available under ISBN 978-3-9820588-4-9. My works revolves around visions, ideas and emotions in past and presence in a figurative-abstract way. I search for freedom, lightness, liveliness and intensity. My studio is a space of experiment, pleasure, frustration and new beginnings. Painting for me has become the way of expressing myself and exploring a world which cannot be explored by words.

ولدت في ألمانيا عام 1953، درس الفنون الجميلة في كاسيل/ ألمانيا وبدأ يحتل مكاناً في المعارض المحلية والعالمية عام 1993. أنا عضو في الجمعية الوطنية للفنون الاحترافية (بي بي كي) وفي الجمعية الوطنية للفنانات الاحترافيات (جي إي دي أو كي). يتوفر فهرسي الأخير " نحو المفتوح" تحت (أي أس بي إن) 9-4-9820588-3-973. تدور أعمالي حول الرؤى، والأفكار، والعواطف حول الماضي والحاضر بطريقة مختصرة رمزية. أبحث عن الحرية، والإشراق، والحيوية، والقوة. الأوستوديو الخاص بي يحتوي على التجربة، والمتعة، وخيبة الأمل، والبدايات الجديدة. الرسومات بالنسبة إلي أصبحت وسيلة للتعبير عن نفسي وطريقة لاستكشاف العالم الذي لن أستطيع اكتشافه بالكلمات.

Earth I, oil colours and oil sticks on canvas, 140x140cm, 2020

Earth II, oil colours and oil sticks on canvas, 150x125cm, 2021

Annemarie Ambrosoli

Annemarie Ambrosoli / ICA (International Certified Artist), was born in South Tyrol. In 2019 she was awarded by A'Design Award & Competition at the Teatro Sociale in Como (Italy) in the category "Art, Crafts and Ready-Made Design". In 2018 she has been nominated in the category of International Artist Award at the World Art Fair Dubai (UAE). In the same year, she received the "Lifetime Achievement Award" from Start Group / Rome at the Award ceremony in the press room of the Chamber of Deputies in Rome (Italy). In 2017 Annemarie Ambrosoli was awarded the second prize at the Gala de l'Art in Montecarlo. Annemarie Ambrosoli in her works expresses her positivity, joy, passion, love, mystery, to reach people's emotional depth. She exhibits internationally.

أنيماري أمبروسولي / أي سي اي (فنانة عالمية معتمدة)، ولدت في جنوب تايرول. في عام 2019 تم تكرينها بواسطة جائزة ومنافسة اي ديزاين في تياترو سوشال في كومبو (ايطاليا) في تصنيف " الفنون والحرف اليدوية والتصميم الجاهز". في عام 2018 تم ترشيحها في تصنيف جائزة الفنان العالمي في معرض الفن العالمي في دبي (الامارات العربية المتحدة). في نفس العام، حصلت على " جائزة الانجاز مدى الحياة" من ستارت جروب/ روما في حفل تسليم الجائزة في غرفة الصحافة بمجلس النواب في روما (إيطاليا). عام 2017 تم تكريم أنيماري أمبروسولي بجائزة للمرة الثانية في جالا دي ال أرت في مومنتيكارلو.تعبر أنيماري أمبروسولي عبر أعمالها عن ايجابيتها، متعتها، شغفها، حبها، غموضها، لتصل إلى عواطف الناس العميقة. هي تعرض أعمالها دولياً.

The Dance of the Hours, 2020, 80x100 cm, oil on canvas

The Waltz of the Flowers, 2020, 80x100 cm, oil on canvas

Erin Starr

In my painting series "Peaceful Reflections" I draw inspiration from the element of water and nature's organic depth of color. Color and light transcend into layers of reflections, contemplating life and our desire for tranquility. Life like water can leave us drifting and floating as we look for answers for peace. We need to preserve our natural environments to create a more peaceful world.

في سلسلة لوحاتي "تأملات مسالمة" قمت برسم الهام من عناصر الماء والعمق العضوي للون الطبيعة الخلاب. اللون والضوء أصبحت طبقات من الانعكاسات، وتأملات للحياة، ورغبة في الهدوء. الحياة كالماء بامكانها تركنا ندور ونطفو باحثين عن الأجوبة عن السلام. علينا الحفاظ على بيئاتنا الطبيعية لنخلق عالماً أكثر سلاماً.

Waters Soothing Rhythm

A Tranquil Place

Jordi Piera

Jordi Piera (Barcelona 1980) is a multidisciplinary artist whose work is mainly focused in the study of light as a sculpture and photography of ephemeral creations. Jordi Piera proposes a man-to-nature dialogue, which ultimately results in the return to a new origin. His artwork offers an emotional journey, transcending the physical world in a process of self-discovery. Elemental geometric shapes create a symbolic language that defines a new generation of primary work. His art is inspired by magical objects created by all types of different cultures throughout human history from both mythology and religion and suggesting a new interpretation in today's world.

جوردي بييرا (برشلونا 1980) هو فنان متعدد الاختصاصات وأعماله تركز بشكل رئيسي على دراسة الضوء على شكل منحوتات وتصوير كابداعات سريعة الزوال. يقترح جوردي بييرا حواراً بين الانسان والطبيعة، والذي يؤدي بشكل لنتائج تعيد إلى أصل جديد بحد أقصى. أعماله الفنية تقدم رحلة عاطفية، تتعدى العالم الحقيقي في عملية استكشاف ذاتي. تخلق الأشكال الهندسي الأولية لغة رمزية تعرف جيلاً جديداً من العمل الأساسي. فنه ملهم بالجمادات السحرية المصنوعة من جميع أنواع الثقافات عبر تاريخ البشرية من بين كل من الأساطير والديانات واقتراح تفسير جديد للعالم اليوم.

Sculpture, Golden Treasure, Mixed Technique, 90 x 75 x 12, 2021

Photography/Installation, Existence, 105 x 70, 2020

Kwon Ji-AN (a.k.a. Solbi)

South Korea | كوريا الجنوبية

Kwon Jian is a South Korean artist who has been a female K-Pop singer since 2006 under the name Solbi and has shown various works such as painting, sculpture, installation, performance, and video art.

كوون جيان هي فنانة من كوريا الجنوبية كانت مغنية كي بوب منذ عام 2006 تحت اسم سولبي وقامت بالعديد من الأعمال الفنية كالرسم، والنحت، والتركيب، والأداء، وفن الفيديو.

Just a Cake - Piece of Hope, Mixed media on canvas, 131x163cm, 2021

Daydream (performance painting)

Johannes Ehemann

Johannes Ehemann on the magic of individuality and blurring the borders of fine arts. The young artist from Germany has given up his professional ice hockey player career to fully concentrate on his true passion, arts. He has developed a unique technique to express his zeitgeist and strikes a chord with collectors of all ages. He photographs natural and authentic situations or people in everyday life. He prints the resulting photos on Polaroid and then crumples them. Each copy takes on a unique character through this process of deformation. He then paints the crumpled structure in oversize with acrylic on a wooden panel in a photo-realistic way. Finally, this painting is milled exactly like the deformed Polaroid template, giving the work an additional tactile feel.

جوهانيس إيهيمان يختص بسحر الفردية وطمس حدود الفنون الجميلة. تخلى هذا الفنان اليافع من ألمانيا مهنته كلاعب هوكي على الجليد ليركز بشكل كامل على شغفه الحقيقي، الفن. قام بتطوير تقنية جديدة للتعبير عن روح العصر وتضرب على وتر حساس لدى هواة جمع التحف من جميع الأعمار. يلتقط صوراً فوتوفرافية للطبيعة وللمواقف الأصيلة أو الناس في حياتهم اليومية. يطبع الصور الناتجة على آلة البولارويد ويقوم بتجعيدها. كل نسخة تأخذ شخصية فريدة عبر عملية التشويه هذه. يقوم بعد ذلك بطباعة الكيان المجعد بشكل أكبر باستخدام مادة الأكريليك على لوح خشبي بشكل صورة فوتوغرافية حقيقية. أخيراً، تصبح هذه الرسمة مدموغة تمامِّ مثل النموذج المجعد بالبولارويد، مما يعطي العمل لمسة محسوسة اضافية.

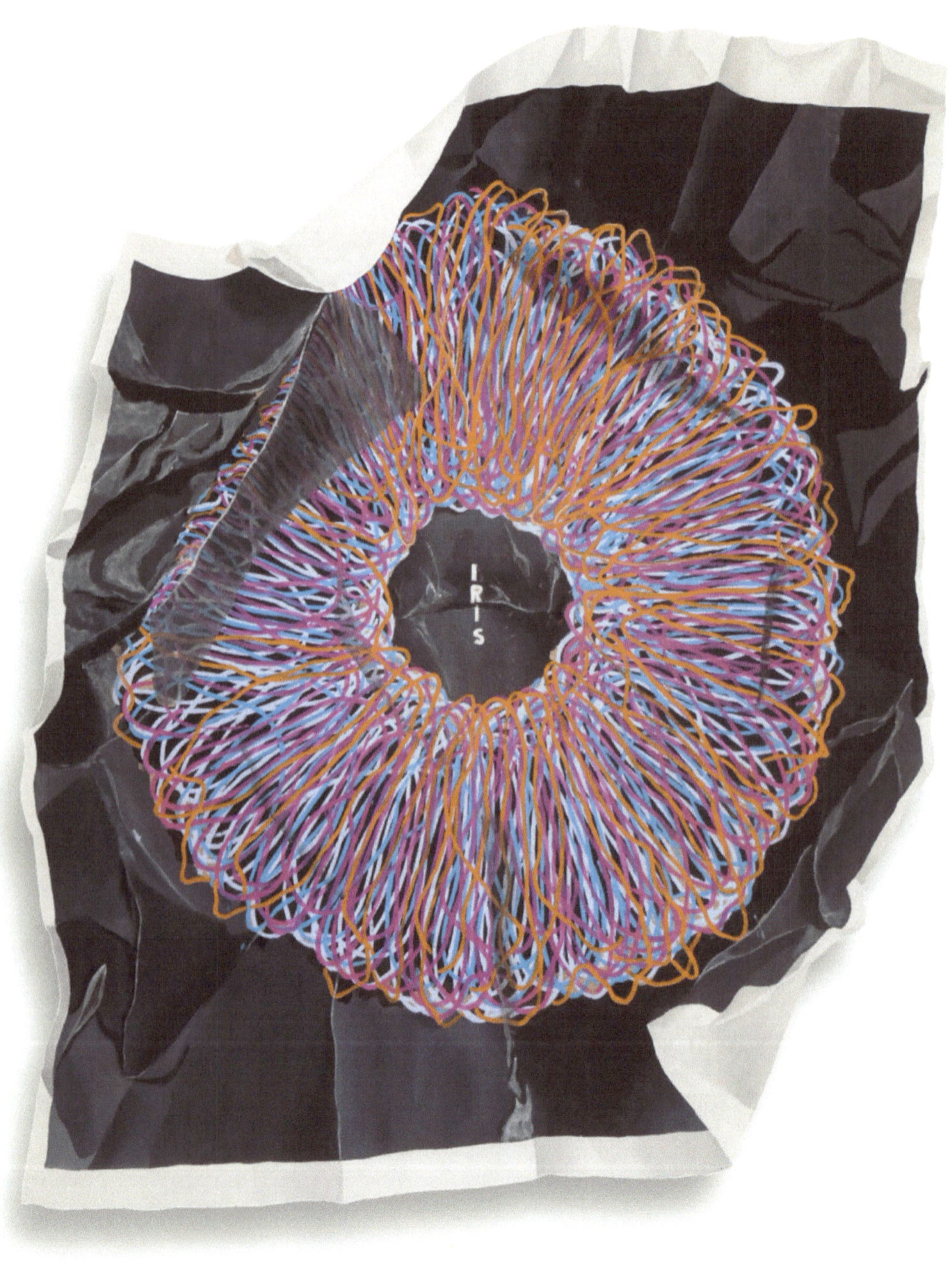

Iris - 2020 - acrylic on wood

Redline - 2021 - acrylic on wood

Cengiz Yatagan

Cengiz Yatağan was born in 1968. He finished his education in Istanbul before moving to Australia, where he was involved in businesses for two years. He has worked in architecture, construction and IT sectors. After specializing in renovation of historic buildings, he focused on arts. Lives and works in Istanbul. I have my own way to express the reflections of my soul by creativity.For me art is a reflection of the mother earth.It's beyond the limits and flows in its own way.

ولد سينجيز ساتاجان عام 1968. أتم دراسته في اسطنبول قبل هجرته لأستراليا، حيث كان مشغولاً بالأعمال لمدة سنتين. عمل في قطاع الهندسة المعمارية، وقطاع أعمال البناء، وقطاع تكنولوجيا المعلومات. قبل تخصصه في تجديد المباني التاريخية، وتركيزه على الفنون. عاش وعمل في اسطنبول. لدي أسلوبي الخاص في التعبير عن انعكاسات روحي بواسطة الإبداع. بالنسبة إلي الفن عبارة عن انعكاس للطبيعة الأم. إنها تتعدى الحدود وتتدفق بطريقتها الخاصة.

Epoxy on metal/100x85x8

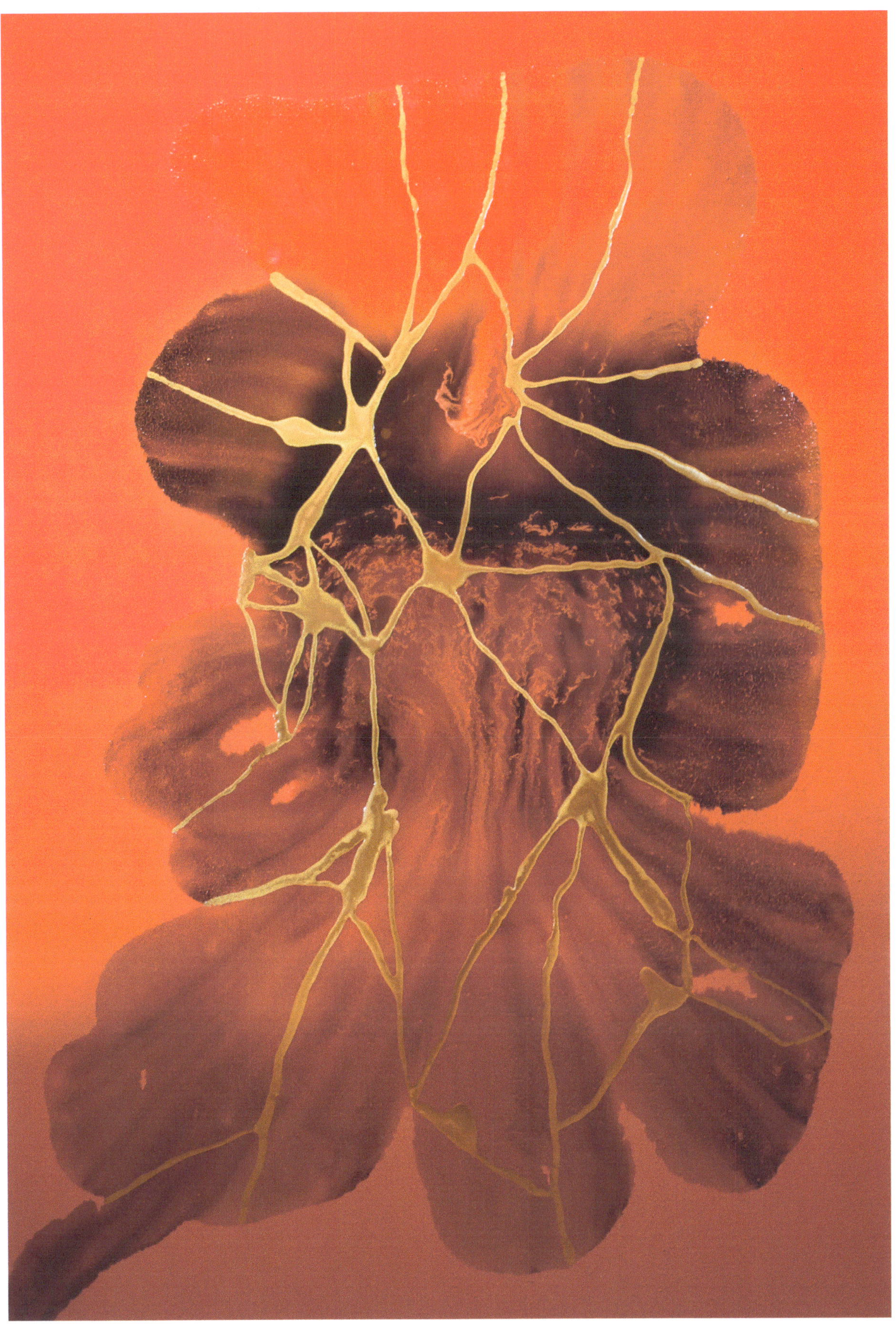

Epoxy on canvas/140x100x4,5

Kat Kleinman

Art allows me an avenue to express my hope for the world. I am a collage artist, focusing on unique floral and succulent compositions, because they symbolize my enthusiasm for using color to bring about positive changes, starting from within. The intention of my work is to make people feel better, even for a moment. I often use dozens of flowers in a single collage, a process that is both meditative and inspirational. The beauty of a floral collage represents healing, because fractions of color combine to create a new cohesive form. I am dedicated to creating art inspired by compassion, meditation and right action.

الفن يعبد لي طريقاً للتعبير عن أملي للعالم. أنا فنان الصاق (كولاج)، أركز على تركيبات وردية نضرة وفريدة من نوعها، لأنها ترمز إلى حماسي لاستخدام الألوان لإحداث تغييرات ايجابية، تبدأ من الداخل.هدف عملي أن أمنح الناس شعوراً أفضل، حتى ولو للحظة. عادةً أستخدم العشرات من الزهور في الكولاج الواحد، عملية تأملية ملهمة. جمال ملصقات الزهور تمثل الشفاء، لأن جزيئات الألوان تتحد لتخلق شكلاً متماسكاً. أنا شخص مثابر نحو خلق فن ملهم بالشفقة، والتأمل والعمل الصحيح.

Mina's Garden

Close To You

Maria Linares Freire

Linares Freire love for geometry and science is the core of her designs, shaping her practice to be the unique art we see today. She is an artist that reflects her views of the universe through fine arts and muralism. One of her paintings was projected on the Moon surface in 2015 by NASA.. WInner of British Woman Artist award July 2019. Winner of the award "Artist of the Future" by Contemporary Art Curator Magazine. Winner of "Artistic Excellence Award" by The Circle Fundation of the Arts. Winner of the "Dante Alighieri International Prize" for the evolution of her career as an artist. As seen in the magazines House and Garden and World of Interiors in 2020.
Collector's Vision International Art Award by Contemporary Art Curator Magazine .
International Prize "Ambassador of Art"
Curators of the Prize are Dr. Francesco Saverio Russo and Salvatore Russo.

حب لينيرز فرير للهندسة والعلوم هو جوهر تصاميمها. تشكل ممارستها فناً فريداً من نوعه نراه اليوم. هي فنانة تعكس نظرتها للكون عبر الفنون الجميلية واللوحات الجدارية. أحد لوحاتها الفنية تم عرضها على سطح القمر عام 2015 بواسطة وكالة ناسا. حازت على جائزة المرأة البريطانية الفنانة في تموز 2019. حائزة على جائزة "فنان المستقبل" من مجلة أمين الفن المعاصر. حائزة على "جائزة التميز الفني" من مؤسسة سيركل للفنون. حائزة على "جائزة دانتي أليغييري الدولية" للثورة التي حققتها في مهنتها كفنانة. كما وجدنا في المجلات جرين وجاردن ووولد أوف انتيريورز عام 2020.

"Evolution I". Acrylic on canvas. 2021

"Utopia-New Earth". Acrylic on canvas. 2020

Somsak Chaituch

Somsak Chaituch (1967) grew up in a small bamboo shed at the hills of Northern Thailand. At 27 Somsak came to the Netherlands to study Art. He got his Master of Fine Arts degree at Twente University in 2003. Somsak is an abstract expressionist painter in a very identical style in brushwork and colour composition. With his lyric between abstract and figurative, Somsak creates music for the eyes. Warm melodies and traditional rhythms of curly shaped lines blend in abstract expression of nature that still refer to the warmth and brilliant colours of his Thai origin. Eastern themes and colours are mixed in western composition and style to give the observers that feeling of sparkling excitement that every powerful artwork must give at first glimpse.

سومساك تشايتش (1967) نشأ في بيت صغير من الخيزران في هضاب شمال تايلاند. في عمر 27 انتقل الى هولندا لدراسة الفن. حصل على درجة الماجستير في الفنون الجميلة من جامعة توينتي عام 2003. يعد سومساك رساما تعبيرياً تجريدياً بنمط مثالي جداً في أعمال الرسم بالريشة وخلط الألوان. بقصته الغنائية التي تجمع التجريدي والمجازي، يخلق سومساك موسيقى للأعين. ألحاناً دافئة وايقاعات تقليدية من مزيج الخطوط مجعدة الشمل كتعبير خالص لطبيعة أصله التايلندي التي ستظل تعكس روعة ودفء تلك الألوان. ألوان وأنماط شرقية مدموجة مع التكوين والأسلوب الغربي لتعطي من يراقبها بشعور تلك الحماسة البراقة التي يعطيها كل عمل فني قوي للوهلة الأولى.

Summer2020#1B, Acrylic on canvas, 200x180cm. 2020

Summer2020#1C, Acrylic on canvas, 200x180cm, 2020

Ursa Schoepper

Ursa Schoepper has a state examination in natural sciences, followed by teaching. She has also a University degree, studies in cultural management, focused on visual arts, new media, at Prof. Dr. Eckart Pankoke, Prof. Dr. Ulrich Krempel and Prof Dr. Michael Bockemühl. Since 2003 she is working as an artist in the field of experimental fine art photography. She exhibits her artworks worldwide and has already received many national and international awards. A digital photography is a light picture and a data image, an icon, a foil of a pictorial perception. Photography is material of different substances. That always means something provisional. Creatively following an artistic idea, I thus develop autonomous photographic images. I create photo autonomous artworks as virtual reality present in realistic reality.

حصلت أوسرا شوير على امتحان الولاية في العلوم الطبيعية، وتابعت بعدها مهنة التدريس. حاصلة أيضاً على درجة جامعية، درست الإدارة الثقافية، وركزت على الفنون المرئية، الإعلام الحديث، يلى يد البروفيسور الدكتور إيكارت بانكوك، والبروفيسور الدكتور أولريتش كرمبل والبروفيسور الدكتور مايكل بوكيمول. منذ عام 2003 وهي تعمل كفنانة في مجال التصوير الفوتوغرافي في الفنون الجميلة. قامت بعرض أعمالها في جميع أنحاء العالم وحازت أيضاً على جوائز دولية ومحلية عديدة. التصوير الفوتوغرافي الرقمي هو عبارة عن صورة ضوئية مكونة من بيانات ضوئية، وأيقونة، رقائق من الادراك التصوري. التصوير الفوتوغرافي هو مادة مكونة من مكونات مختلفة. وهو ما يعني دائماً شيئاً مؤقتاً. اتباع فكرة الفنان بشكل مبدع، لذلك أقوم بتصوير صور فوتوغرافية مستقلة خاصة بي. أقوم بأعمال فنية من صور فوتوغرافية كحقيقة افتراضية تمثل في حقيقة واقعية.

Desert, Color Pigment on Aludibond, 54 x 140 cm, 2020.

Canyons, Color Pigment on Aludibond, 50 x 75 cm, 2020.

Anne Felicie Nickels

I am an artist driven by the materials with which I work. I am constantly learning and exploring the limits of my medium. My ambition is to continually develop and improve each technique I employ. For example, I love both the beauty of glass and the challenge it proves to be. In my opinion, art is a method of communication that enriches both the artist and the viewer. My art centers on subject matter close to my heart and I am most thankful that life has given me the opportunity to express myself artistically.

أنا فنانة تدفعني المواد التي أعمل بها. أنا أتعلم وأستكشف حدود محيطي بشكل ثابت. طموحي هو تطوير وتحسين كل تقنية أستخدمها بشكل مستمر. على سبيل المثال، أحب كلاً من جمال الزجاج وتحدي اثبات وجوده. برأيي، الفن طريقة للتواصل تثري كلا من الفنان والمضطلع الناظر. فني يتمركز حول موضوع قريب من قلبي وأنا في غاية الامتنان لما منحتني إياه الحياة. من فرصة لأعبر عن نفسي فنيا.

ScrapArt Skanör #6, Kiln Formed Glass, 41 x 24 x 8 cm

ScrapArt Öresund #7, Kiln Formed Glass, 44 x 22 x 8 cm

Eric Hubbes

My images arise in a storm of thoughts and emotions that manifest themselves in forms and fractals, which I combine into a composition. In my pictures I let my subconscious run free. With the geometric and fractal patterns in my pictures, I also show my interest in natural sciences. At the same time, I am also fascinated by psychology and the influence of the subconscious on our actions. I like to imagine when I paint that I communicate with the universe or that the universe sends me messages that I process in my pictures. I have given my paintings the name "Grübel Bilder" or "Muse-paintings" because I transfer my self-doubts into something life-affirming and make art come out of it.

تشرق صوري من عاصفة من الأفكار والعواطف والتي تتجلى في أشكال وفرتكلات، أجمعها معاً في مركب. في صوري أسمح لعقلي الباطن بأن يجري بحرية. عن طريق الأنماط الهندسية والفركتالية في صوري، أظهر أيضاً اهتمامي بالعلوم الطبيعية. في الوقت ذاته، أنا أيضاً مفتونة بعلم النفس وأثر العقل الباطن على أفعالنا. أحب أن أتخيل أثناء الرسم بأنني أتواصل مع الكون أو بأن الكون يرسل لي رسائل أنفذها في صوري. أعطيت لوحاتي اسم "جروبيل بايلدر" أو "لوحات ميوز" لأنني أحقل شكوكي الشخصية إلى شيء يؤكد على الحياة وأصنع منه فناً.

The scholar

Brigitta Westphal

Brigitta Westphal is born in Germany. A thorough education in painting and the graphic arts are the basis for the artist to realize her ideas effectively. Human and nature stand as main subjects in the center of her oeuvre. Therefore, her individual focus deriving from subjective biographical elements forms the artist`s works. Since 1986, transferring world literature into adequate picturesque works is a special challenge to the artist. Lectures in France, Germany and USA:

Subject: "Literature and its Transference into Painting in the View of an Artist".

Brigitta Westphal taught the techniques of etching and painting in Riad, Saudi Arabia:

2012 Painting workshop, 2015 Graphic workshop.

By highly regarded expositions in Germany, USA and in other European countries (especially Italy) her oeuvre became known.

ولدت بريجيتي ويستفال في ألمانيا. التعليم المكتمل في الرسم وفنون الجرافيك هو الأساس في ادراك الفنانة لأفكارها بشكل أكثر فعالية. يشكل الانسان والطبيعة مواضيع رئيسية في صميم أعمالها الفنية. لذلك، تشتق تركيزها الفردي من عناصر سيرتها الذاتية مما يشكل أعمالها الفنية. منذ عام 1986، شكل تحويل الأدب العالمي إلى أعمال فنية مناسبة تحدياً خاصاً للفنان. محاضرات في فرنسا، ألمانيا، والولايات المتحدة الأمريكية:

الموضوع: "الأدب وتحويله إلى لوحات في نظر الفنان".

درست بريجيتي ويستفال تقنيات في النقش والرسم في الرياض، المملكة العربية السعودية:

ورشة عمل للرسم 2012، ورشة عمل للجرافيك 2015. عبر المعارض المرموقة في ألمانيا، وأمريكا، ودول أوروبية أخرى (وبالأخص ايطاليا) عرفت أعمالها الإبداعية الفنية.

"Silence farewell I" to a Poem of Brigitta Westphal, Oil/Oil pastel, 40 x 40 cm

"Silence farewell III" to a Poem of Brigitta Westphal, Oil/Oil pastel, 40 x 40 cm

Belle Roth

My work is inspired by architecture; simple lines that do not conform to standard design or configuration. My compositions are intentionally deconstructed to obtain a multifaceted characteristic; each exploring different experiences and cultures that have inspired my brush. I unveil my life experiences through my interpretation of colors, textures, and details. I create my style of work by infusing acrylic paint with mixed-media techniques, all with consideration of the environment that surrounds me, including influential elements from my Southeast Asian roots.

ألهمت أعمالي بفن الهندسة المعمارية؛ خطوط بسيطة لا تتفق مع التصميم أو التكوين القياسي. أقوم بتفكيك مؤلفاتي بطريقة مقصودة للوصول إلى خواص متعددة الأوجه؛ كل منها يستكشف تجارب وثقافات مختلفة مما يلهم ريشتي. أنا أكشف النقاب عن تجارب حياتي بواسطة أداء الألوان، والقوامات، والتفاصيل. أصنع أسلوبي في العمل بواسطة غرس ألوان الأكريليك بتقنيات وسائط مختلطة، كل ذلك مع الأخذ بالبيئة المحيطة بي بعين الاعتبار، والتي تشمل عناصر مؤثرة من جذور أصلي الجنوب آسيوية.

Denver Day 2 - Acrylic on Canvas , 48 x 48, 2020

Cairo Day 8 - Acrylic on Canvas , 60 x 48, 2020

Andre Schoots

The time is constant changing. André Schoots welcomes the beholder into the tableaus he paints to contemplate, triggering thoughts and emotions. The two colorful paintings presented here are reflections on times gone by. A view from the back seat of a fifties VW Beetle. A lady driver behind an extravagant Chevrolet Impala. She just passed a girl on a bicycle as seen in the rearview mirror. Is it all symbolic? Like the painting about forgiveness, where a road sign flakes off to give a new direction, one off embrace. Schoots is an emerging artist who followed two tracks in terms of education and profession. He has been working as an embryologist. His oil paintings merited several international certificates and awards.

الوقت يتغير بشكل ثابت. يرحب أندري سكوتس الناظر إلى رسماته الفنية التي يرسمها ليحفزه على التفكير، ويحفز أفكاره وعواطفه. اللوحتان الرائعتان المعروضتان تمثل تأملات في أوقات مضت. نافذة من المقعد الخلفي من الخمسينيات وزمن البيتل. فتاة تسوق سيارة شيفروليه إمبالا باهظة الثمن. عبرت بجانب فتاة تبدل على دراجة هوائية كما هو ملحوظ من المشهد الظاهر في المرآة. هل هذا كله رمزي؟ مثل اللوحات التي تتحدث عن التسامح، عندما تشير لافتة الطريق لاتجاه جديد، عناق لمرة واحدة. سكوتس فنان ناشئ سلك مسارين أحدهما التعليم والآخر المهنة. كان يعمل في عالم الأجنة. لوحاته الزيتية استحقت العديد من الجوائز وشهادات التقدير العالمية.

Marjolaine in Mayenne, oil on canvas, 60x80 cm

Forgiveness, oil on canvas, 60x80 cm

Marco Benedetti

Switzerland | سويسرا

Marco Benedetti is a Swiss Artist and Professional Photographer with Italian roots. He has been active behind the camera since as early as 1990. He loves using available light always when possible, putting more importance to the excellent management of his analogue and digital cameras than to external props and photo retouching. Apart from using high end photo technique, Marco Benedetti creates Artworks with analogue techniques like wet plate (glass) and pin hole cameras, mixing photography, painting and collage. He is an award-winning perfectionist, uncompromising on resources to achieve his visions in the highest quality possible. His photos and mixed media projects were awarded more than 100 times in the last 5 years: receiving international awards like "Outstanding Achievement", "Merit of Excellence" and "Honorable Mention".

ماكرو بينيديتي فنان سويسري ومصور فوتوغرافي محترف من أصول ايطالية. بدأ نشاطه خلف الكاميرا منذ بداية عام 1990. يحب استخدام الاضاءة المتاحة عندما يسمح الأمر بذلك، ويعطي أهمية أكبر للتميز الاداري لمنظوره وكاميرته الرقمية مقارنة بالدعائم الخارجية وتعديل الصورة. بعيداً عن استخدامه تقنيات تصوير ذات جودة عالية، صنع ماكرو بينيديتي أعمالاً فنية بتقنيات التصوير التناظري (التقليدي) مثل قطعة الزجاج المبللة وكاميرات ثقت الدبوس، ودمج بين التصوير الفوتوغرافي، والرسم، والكولاج. هو محترف تم تكريمه بعدة جوائز، متشبث بالموارد ليصل لرؤاه بأفضل جودة ممكنة. تم تكريم صوره ومشاريعه الاعلامية المختلفة أكثر من 100 مرة في السنوات الخمسة الماضية: حصل على جوائز عالمية مثل "الانجاز المتميز"، و"استحقاق التميز"، و"الشرفية.

Silence To Tell You

Decomposition And Metamorphosis

Berta Jayo

Berta Jayo was born in Santander, Spain. She has a degree in Fine Arts from the University of the Basque Country. She did postgraduate and master at Chelsea College of Art and Design in London and continued her training at ISCP in New York. In her works she shows an innovative art, far from stereotypes. She is considered a multidisciplinary conceptual artist whose line is marked by codes of a free and surprising nature. Other facets are architectural designs and artist's books. Her works have been shown in many countries in exhibitions and museums such as The Chill Concept Miami, Bronx Museum NY, CAC Málaga, MAS, Gugenheim Bilbao, Tate Modern, Reina Sofía, MoMa, Louvre Paris.

ولدت بيرتا جايو في سانتاندر، اسبانيا. حصلت على شهادة الفنون الجميلة من جامعة باسكو كنتري. أنجزت تعليمها العالي ودرجة الماجستير في كلية شيلسي للفن والتصميم في لندن وأكملت تدريبها في "أي أس سي بي" في نيويورك. تظهر في أعمالها فناً ابداعياً، بعيداً عن الأفكار التقليدية النمطية. تعتبر فنانة خيال متعددة الاختصاصات في مسار ذو طبيعة حرة ومدهشة في ذات الوقت. وفي جوانب أخرى من التصميم الهندسي المعماري وكتب الفنانين. عرضت أعمالها في دول عدة في مختلف المعارض والمتاحف مثل ذا تشيلي كونسبت في ميامي، ومتحف برونكس في نيويورك، وسي اي سي مالاجا، وإم اي اس، وجوجينهيم بيلباو، وتاتي موديرن، ورينا صوفيا، وموما، واللوفر في باريس.

Magazines & Poverty, 20x30cm. 2020

Passion Daily

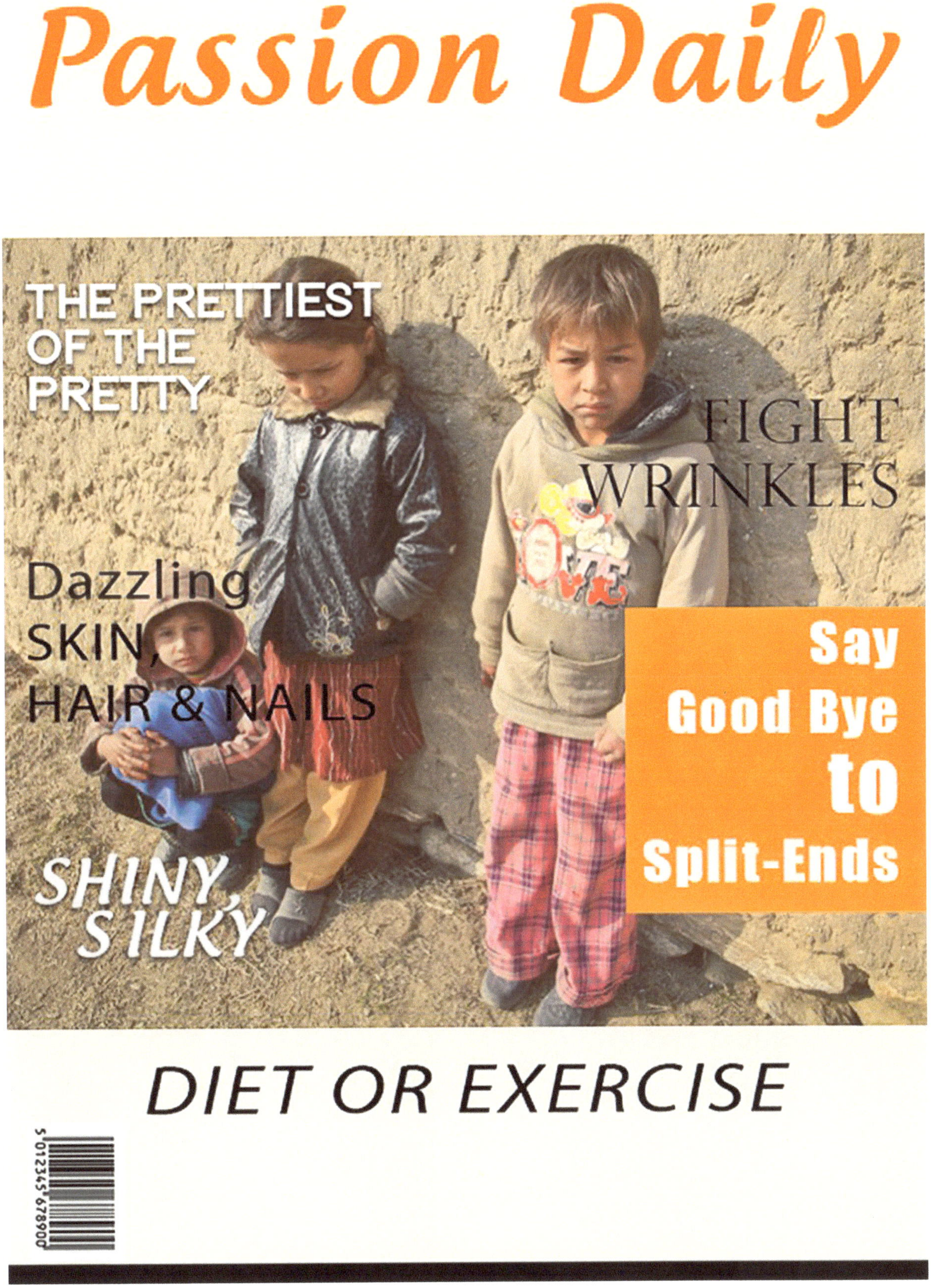

Earth II, oil colours and oil sticks on canvas, 150x125cm, 2021

Danny Johananoff

Danny Johananoff, wildly known for his blurred and impressionist style, is exhibiting in Italy, Tokyo, Shanghai, Hong Kong, NY and Miami. Danny is photographing for over 50 years, fascinated by the different cultures, nature and images out there. He describes his technique as "Painting" with the camera, using slow speed and camera movement method. He leaves his mind and soul open to receive whatever calls him out there. Drawn to the amazing world of insects and Macro photography, he became fond of those little creatures he can see through the lens, not always available for the naked eye. Danny loves sharing his different style with the hope that more will enjoy his particular view.

داني جوهانانوف، عرف بشكل واسع بأسلوبه الانطباعي والغير واضح، تعرض أعماله في ايطاليا، طوكيو، شنجهاي، هونج كونج، نيويورك، ميامي. يمارس داني التصوير الفوتوغرافي لأكثر من 50 عاماً، مسحورة بعدة ثقافات، والطبيعة، والصور من العالم الخارج. يصف طريقته الفنية بـ"الرسم" بواسطة الكاميرا، يستخدم طريقة التصوير المتحرك والسرعة البطيئة. يدع عقله وروحه مفتوحين لاستقبال أي اتصالات قادمة إليه من الخارج. انجذب إلى عالم الحشرات والتصوير الفوتوغرافي الدقيق (مايكرو)، أصبح مغرماً بتلك الكائنات الدقيقة التي يمكنه رؤيتها في عدساته، والتي لا تكون واضحة دائماً للعين المجردة. يحب داني مشاركة أسلوبه الفريد على أمل أن يستمتع المزيد برؤيته الخاصة.

"Carrying the Night", Vietnam, 2020

"Snatch the Goat", Kyrgyzstan 2018

Aomi Kikuchi

I make sculptures, wall pieces and garments using textiles and found objects to explore Japanese aesthetics and the philosophy of Buddha. They are "Wabi-Sabi", the beauty found in imperfections, and "Mono-no-aware", the feeling of sympathy for changing or perishing phenomena or substances. Closely related to the philosophy of Buddha, these can be summarized in three key words: impermanence, insubstantiality, and suffering. My work addresses infinity as the succession of fleeting and brittle activities. I create art to inspire dialogue and reflection on these concepts through materials and aesthetic philosophies. With freedom and flexibility, I combine acquired knowledge and experiment. I actively use scraps that come from both my working practice and the environment around me.

أنا أصنع تماثيلاً، وقطع الحائط، والملابس باستخدام المنسوجات والأشياء التي أجدها لاستكشاف الثقافة اليابانية والفلسفة البوذية. إنها "وابي- سابي"، الجمال الذي نجده في العيوب، و"مانو- نو- أوير"، الشعور بالتعاطف نحو تغيير أو هلاك المواد أو ظواهر. وهذا يتعلق بشكل وطيدبالفلسفة البوذية، والتي يمكن تلخيصها بثلاثة كلمات مفتاحية: الثبات، والدهاء، والمعاناة. يعالج عملي اللانهاية على أنها سلسلة من الأنشطة العابرة والهشة. أقوم بصناعة الفن الملهم للحوار والتفكير في هذه المفاهيم من خلال المواد والفلسفات الجمالية. عبر الحرية والمرونة، أجمع بين المعرفة المكتسبة والخبرة. أستخدم القصاصات بشكل فعال والتي أستوحيها من ممارستي العملية والبيئة المحيطة بي.

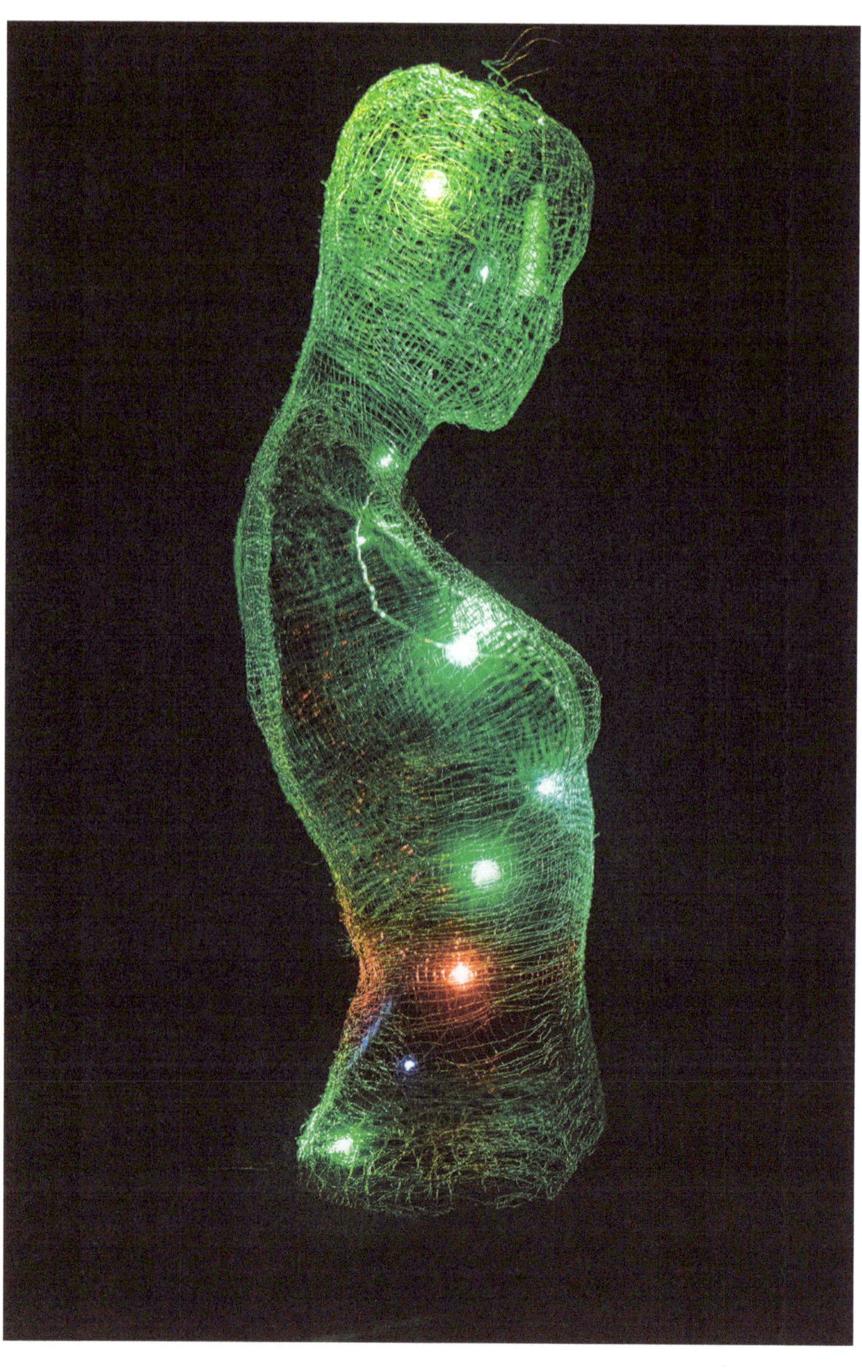

Cage of Life

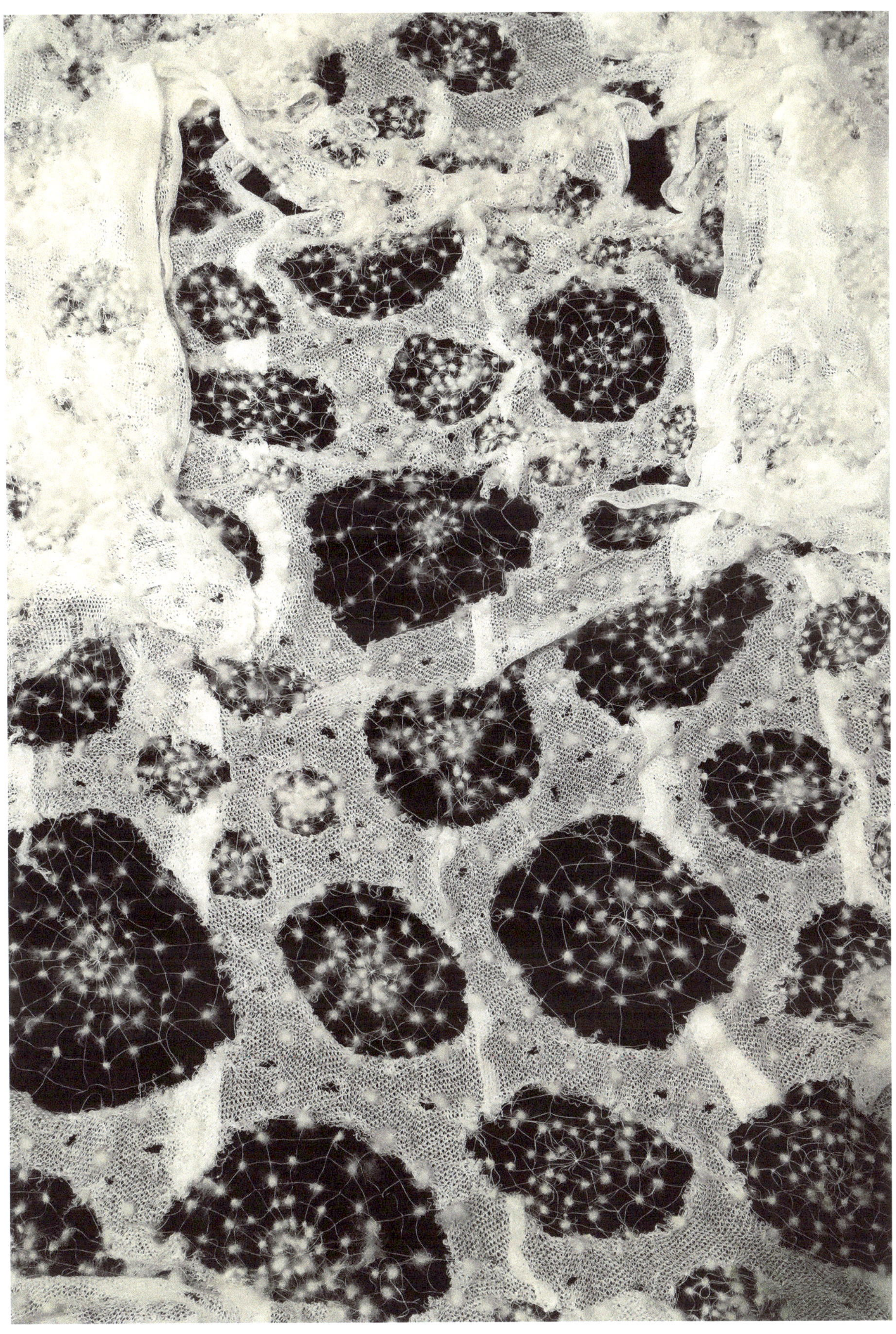

Transition

Duygu Kıvanc

Duygu Kivanc is an artist who has shown her work at the United Nations, SOHO, Chelsea in New York, Alexandria, McLean and Fairfax in the Northern Virginia/Washington DC area as well as internationally in various countries. Duygu has an Associates Degree in Textiles. She considers her participation in the Art Students' League (open studio programs) in New York has influenced her development style in art. Especially, Knox Martin's instruction on abstraction has very strong influence. Kivanc presents works inspired by her three years in Bhutan in narrative text and mixed-media pictures totaling 38 pages, making this a brief art book. Lives and works in Turkey and in the United States.

دويجو كيفانك هي فنانة عرضت أعمالها في الأمم المتحدة، سوهو، شلسي في نيويورك، الاسكندرية، مكلين وفيرفاكس في منطقة شمال فرجينيا/واشنطون دي سي بالاضافة إلى دول عدة أخرى عالمياً. حصلت دويجو على درجة الزمالة في المنسوجات والملابس. تعتبر مشاركتها في رابطة طلاب الفنون (برامج الأستوديو المفتوح) في نيويورك قد أثرت في تطوير أسلوبها في الفن. بالأخص، كان لتعليمات نوكس مارتن في التعبير التجريدي أثراً قوياً جداً. تقدم كيفانكس أعمالاً ملهمة بسنواتها الثلاثة في بوتان في النص السردي واصور الوسائط المتعددة بمجموع 38 صفحة، والذي يجعله كتاباً فنياً ملخصاً مختصراً. تعيش وتعمل في تركيا والولايات المتحدة الأمريكية.

Daydreaming

İstinye İstanbul

Tjeerd Doosje

Tjeerd Doosje was born on april 8th 1966, Harderwijk, the Netherlands and is a self-taught and international awarded portraitphotographer and retoucher. After he graduated from highschool he studied mathematics and chemistry at the Hogeschool Utrecht to become a teacher. He's still a mathteacher at a highschool in Almere and around 2010, he discovered portrait photography. His photos have been finalist for The Celeste Contemporary Art Prize 2016 (London) and twice in The Global Art Awards 2018 (Dubai) and 2020 (Shanghai). He was also several times a runner up (nominated) for the Fine Art Photography Awards (2018, 2019, 2020). He received international prizes, among them Andrea Mantegna Prize (Mantova, 2017) and International Prize Velázquez (Barcelona, 2019).

ولد تجيرد دوسج في الثامن من ابريل عام 1966، هاردرفيك، في هولندا وهو عصامي ومصور بورتريه ومنقح ملابس تم تكريمه عالمياً. بعد تخرجه من المدرسة الثانوية درس الرياضيات والكيمياء في مدرسة هوج أوتريخت ليصبح معلماً. ولا يزال معلم رياضيات في ثانوية ألميري وفي عام 2010، اكتشف التصوير الفوتوغرافي الشخصي. صوره وصلت للتصفيات النهائية في جائزة سيلسيت للفن المعاصر 2016 (لندن) ومرتين في لجائزة الفن العالمي 2018 (دبي) و2020 (شنجهاي). ترشح أيضاً لعدة مرات لجوائز للتصوير الفوتوغرافي والفنون الجميلة (2018،2019،2020). حاز على جوائز عالمية، من بينها جتئزة أندريا مانتيجنا (مانتوفا، 2017) وجائزة فنزويلا العالمية (برشلونا، 2019).

Merlin (0101) - Photograph - 60 cm x 40 cm (h x w) - 2020 (Model: Merlin Sen)

Anoek (0109) - Photograph - 60 cm x 40 cm (h x w) - 2019

Caspar Baum

Caspar Baum has presented his work in private and public spaces over the last three decades, including some significant solo shows globally. His work is influenced by the light and structure of the objects. It plays with shadows and illumination, background and front, separates into layers and re-composes those to a new imagination taking the observer into a silent sensitive environment. When he is asked to find similarities to his work in other areas of art he compares his work with music, with the waves of sounds and changing instrumentation.

Caspar Baum has received many awards and his works are represented in private and public collections around the globe.

عرض كاسبر باوم أعماله في الأماكن الخاصة والعامة عبر الثلاثة عقود الماضية، والتي تتضمن بعض العروض الفردية حول العالم. تأثر عمله بالإضاءة والهيكلة للأشياء. إنها تلعب بالظلال والإنارة، الخلفية والأمامية، تفصلها إلى طبقات وتعيد تكوينها لخيالات جديدة تأخذ المتأمل إلى بيئة حساسة صامتة. عندما يطلب منه ايجاد أوجه شبه لعمله في مساحات فن أخرى يقوم بمقارنة عمله بالموسيقى، مع موجات الصور وتغيرات الآلات الموسيقية. حاز كاسبر باوم على العديد من الجوائز وعرضت أعماله في المعارض الخاصة والعامة جول العالم.

Pacific Paintings Nr 1, Oil on Canvas, 2020

City Paintings, New York, Oil on Canvas, 2019

Angelika Prapa

Angelika Prapa was born in Graz, Austria, and was raised in Thessaloniki, Greece. After her studies in Comparative Literature and Psychology, she followed a professional career in writing and editing didactic and psychological-medical Books. Her lifelong interest in painting led her to the department of Fine and Applied Arts of Aristoteles University of Thessaloniki in Greece, where she graduated withe excellence . She participated in many Exhibitions and her works are in Museums and private Collections.

ولدت أنجيليكا برابا في جراز، النمسا، زتربت في ثيسالونيكي، اليونان. بعد دراستها الأدب المقارن والفلسفة، التحقت بمهنة الكتابة والتعديل التوجيهي وكتب الطب النفسي. اهتمامها الأبدي بالرسم قادها لقسم الفنون الجميلة والتطبيقية في جامعة أرسطو، اليونان، حيثما تخرجت بدرجة امتياز. شاركت في العديد من المعارض وعرضت أعمالها في المتاحف والمعارض الخاصة.

Fly with me. Oil on linen, 160x160cm

Falling Angels. Oil on linen, 190x160cm

Yaroslava Liseeva

We live in the world where everything is inconstant and changing, moving and interconnecting. In my works I appeal to emotional and spiritual dimensions. Nowadays when our minds are overloaded with tons of information, social networks, news, it is very important just to make a stop and to open the eyes and see the world around, listen to it, feel it. We can see and feel so many things, when we tune ourselves for that. Focusing on landscape images I try to create dynamic, voluminous and flowing world. The trees, the oceans, the lakes, wind, fire… The real things. But if we observe these phenomena with all our senses, they open for us their metaphorical essence and acquire universal, mythological characteristics.

نعيش في عالم كل شيء فيه غير ثابت ويتغير، يتحرك ويترابط. في العديد من الأعمال أطلب الأبعاد العاطفية والروحية. هذه الأيام وعقولنا مثقلة بالأطنان من المعلومات، والشبكات الاجتماعية، والأخبار، من الضروري أن نتوقف ونفتح أعيننا ونرى العالم من حولنا، نستمع إليه، نشعر به. نستطيع رؤية واحساس الكثير من الأشياء، عنما نعود أنفسنا على ذلك. أحاول خلق ديناميكية بالتركيز على المناظر الطبيعية، عالم ضخم ومتدفق. الأشجار، المحيطات، البحيرات، الريح، النار... الأشياء الحقيقية. لكن لو لاحظنا هذه الظواهر بجميع حواسنا، سيفتحون لنا جوهرهم المجازي ونحصل على العالمية، الخصائص الأسطورية.

The Flow of Life. The Beginning

The Three Destinies

Joey Cruz Margarejo

Joey's a self taught abstract acrylic on canvas artist, always believe that artist should be FREE, I love it when people take a deep look, criticizing, analyzing and asked is this Art? It means he touched their hearts and soul. Joey loves using only 2 brushes that speaks a thousand words, touched a thousand hearts and feel a thousand emotions.

يعد جووي فناناً عصامياً في التجريد بالأكريليك على اللوحات القماشية، يؤمن دوماً بأن الفنان يجب أن يكون حراً، أحب ذلك عندما [اخذ الناس نظرة عميقة، ينتقدوا، يحللوا، ويسألوا هل هذا فن؟ ذلك يعني أنه قد لمس قلوبهم وروحهم. يحب جووي استخدام فرشاتين تتكلمان ألف كلمة، تلمس ألفاً من القلوب وتحس ألفاً من العواطف.

My mother's Lullaby 2, acrylic on canvas 40H X 30W in. Year:2019 this is a part of a series dedicated to my mother who passed away the night before my show in Vancouver BC

My mother's Lullaby 3, acrylic on canvas 40H X 30W in. Year 2019 3rd.piece dedicated to my mother who passed away the night before my show in Vancouver Bc

Max Werner

Born in Ghent Belgium. Studied Fine Art at the Slade School of art in London UCL University. Later taught etching in the same school.Then moved to Buenos Aires Argentina for 6 years where he completed a body of work about Argentina landscapes and the gaucho-cattle world of that country. Max now lives and works in Wyoming, USA. His work can be seen in many public and private collections in Europe, South America, Japan and the USA.

ولد في جينت بلجيكا. درس الفنون الجميلة في مدرسة سليد للفنون في جامعة يو سي إل لندن. وقام بتدريس النقش لاحقاً في نفس المدرسة. بعد ذلك انتقل إلى بوينس ايرس في الأرجنتين لستة سنوات وهناك أكمل جزءاً من عمله عن مناظر الأرجنتين الطبيعية وعن عالم جاوتشو-كاتل في تلك الدولة. يعيش ماكس الآن ويعمل في وايومنغ، الولايات المتحدة الأمريكية. مكن مشاهدة أعماله في المجمعات العامة والخاصة في أوروبا، أمريكا الجنوبية، اليابان، والولايات المتحدة الأمريكية.

"Petrified Ghosts". Acrylic/canvas. 38" X 18"

"Yellowstone National Park" 21,5" X 34"

Amalia Borin

The cultural roots of Amalia Borin fade in the misty meanders of the Po delta, where she was born and grew up until she moved near Bologna, where she attended the Academy of Fine Arts under the direction of Concetto Pozzati. Her colored ribbons sublimate the rivers and canals of her ancestral land, as they encrypt that chromatic poem of light written by Nature into the very code which is the quintessence of her style's symbolic magnetism. Her choice to paint sculptures is the result of her personal artistic research and growth, which culminated into something or somewhere utterly new, where her ancestral desire to create figurative art finally weds to her admiration for abstractism and action painting. (Patrick Dennis).

الجذور الثقافية لأماليا بورين تغيب في التشوهات الضبابية لبو الدلتا، المكان الذي ولدت وتربت فيه حتى انتقلت منهم قريب بولوجنا، أينما التحقت بأكاديمية الفنون الجميلة تحت توجيه كونسيتو بوزاتي. شرائطها الملونة تصعد الأنهار والجداول في أراضي أجدادها، حيث يقومون بتشفير تلك القصيدة اللونية للضوء التي تكتبها الطبيعة في نفس الشفرة التي تمثل جوهر الجذب الرمزي لأسلوبها. اختيارها لتلوين التماثيل نتيجة لبحثها وغوها الفني الشخصي، والذي يبلغ أوجه نحو شيء أو مكان جديد تماماً، أينما تكون رغبتها الموروثة في صنع فن بليغ أخيراً متزاوجة مع اعجابها بالتجريد والرسم العملي.

(باتريك دينيس)

Ethics 2016. Painted Acrylic Clay

Ethics 2018. Painted Acrylic Clay

Jaime Jose

Was born in Monterrey, Nuevo Leon, Mexico in 1942. At a very young age he started experimenting with drawing .It is in 1981 when he became fully dedicated to his artwork experimenting with color and form. During 1991 he traveled to Tours, France in search for new ways to confront and enrich his artwork participating indifferent expositions and receiving "Toulouse- Hispanic Silver Award". He has ever since been in a constant search of evolution receiving awards from Spain, Italy and his native Mexico and Latin America. Today Jaime Jose is considered a Latinamerican figurative artist. He has more than 33 individual exhibitions and 200 collective ones in North, Central and South America, Europe and Asia.

ولد في مونتيري، نويفو ليون، المكسيك عام 1942. في عمر صغير بدأ تجريب الرسم. أصبح مثابراً بشكل كامل نحو أعماله الفنية التجريبية مع اللون والشكل في عام 1981. خلال عام 1991 سافر إلى تورز، فرنسا في بحث عن سبل جديدة لمواجهة وإثراء أعماله الفنية المشاركة بالمعارض الغير عادية واستلام "جائزة تولوس- هيسبانيك الفضية". منذ ذلك الحين وهو في بحث ثابت عم الصورة واستلم جوائز من اسبانيا، ايطاليا، وبلده المكسيك وأمريكا اللاتينية. يعتبر اليوم جيمي جوس اليوم فناناً تشكيلياً من أمريكا اللاتينية. لديه الآن أكثر من 33 معرض فردي و 200 وحدة مجموعة في الشمال، الوسط والجنوب في أمريكا وأوروبا وآسي.

Busquemos la Felicidad

Los Pétalos de la Rosa

Bo Song

I was born in 1968 in Korea and I am currently working in Unjung-dong in Korea. I studied at Dan-kook Graduate Art School,Korea. BA in Oil Painting, at Oakland University,Michigan,USA. I showcase my art through the concept of energy from nature and human spirits which may not be seen with the naked eye, however those are principles we all surely come from and surrounded by us. To be able to express nature's complex such as; Earth, Water, Fire, Wind, Space which is a fathomless beauty. I have been expressing that just way with my colors and shapes. Painting is my language, and it has become a part of me - it is my life.

ولدت في عام 1968 في كوريا وأعمل حالياً في أونجونج دونج في كوريا. درست في دان-كوك وتخرجت من مدرسة الفنون، كوريا. بي اي في الرسم الزيتي، في جامعة أوكلاند، ميشيجين، الولايات المتحدة الأمريكية. عرضت فني عبر مفهوم الطاقة من أرواح الطبيعة والإنسان والتي لا يمكن رؤيتها بالعين المجردة، بالرغم من أنها مبادئ أتينا منها ومحاطون بها بالتأكيد. لأستطيع التعبير عن تعقيد الطبيعة على سبيل المثال؛ الأرض، الماء، النار، الريح، الفضاء أينما الجمال لا يسبر غوره. كنت دوماً أعبر عن ذلك بألواني وأشكالي. الرسم هي لغتي، وأصبح جزءاً مني- هو حياتي.

All Things in Nature, 2020,Oil on Canvas, 150x75cm

Interconnected, 2020,Oil on Canvas,150x75cm

Kench Lott Weathers

الولايات المتحدة الأمريكية | United States

Kench Lott Weathers is an American artist residing in Savannah, Georgia. Primarily a three-dimensional artist, he creates art across many disciplines. Some of his influences consist of the Minimalists, Op-artists and Constructivists. He received his Bachelor of Fine Arts at Savannah State University and a Master of Fine Arts - emphasis in sculpture- at Georgia Southern University. His installations make use of the rooms interior and architectural layout by incorporating mixed media structures in a nontraditional format; making use of the corners, ceiling and floor. The materials used range from steel, wood and light. His work is not a critique of contemporary society, but an escape from it. His installations challenge the viewers sense of space and depth.

كينتش لوت ويذرز هو فنان أمريكي مقيم في سافانا، جورجيا. بالأساس فنان ثلاثي الأبعاد، يصنع الفن عبر تخصصات عدة. أحد تأثيراته يتكون من الحدود الدنيا، فناني الأوب، والبنائين. استلم درجة البكالوريوس في الفنون الجميلة من جامعة ولاية سافانا ودرجة الماستر في الفنون الجميلة – التركيز في النحت من جامعة جورجيا الجنوبية. تماثيله تستخدم في التصميم الداخلي للغرف والمخططات المعمارية عن طريق دمج وسائط هيكلية متعددة في شكل غير تقليدي: يجعل الزوايا، الأسقف، والأرضيات ذات استخدامات معتبرة. تتنوع المواد المستخدمة بين الحديد، الخشب، والأضوية. عمله ليس نقداً للمجتمع المعاصر، بل هروبٌ منه. تخلق منشآته تحدياً لاحساس المشاهد بالعمث والمساحة.

Simplex Illusio, 2020 (welded steel)

Mindful Escapism, 2018 (welded steel)

Frank Mann

The repetition of loose circular structures in Mann's process and the material engagement with paint applied to canvas has become a poetic language occupying the energy of life made visible. His paintings are the structural signs of energy, and in that mode, they work as gorgeous signs of drama played out by color and shape evocative of art's vast and revelatory power for the possibility of transcendental experience. As Mark Rothko once said, "I do not believe that there was ever a question of being abstract or representational. It is really a matter of ending this silence and solitude, of breathing and stretching one's arms again." Mann's paintings do just that. Franklin Sirmans, Curator of Contemporary Art, Los Angeles County Museum of Art.

تكرار الهياكل الدائرية الهشة في عملية مان وارتباط المادة مع الرسم المطبق على اللوحات أصبح لغة شعرية تشغل طاقة الحياة وتجعلها ظاهرة. تعد لوحاته علامات هيكلية للطاقة، وفي تلك الحالة، تعمل كعلامات رائعة من الدراما التي يلعبها اللون والشكل الذي يستحضر قوة الفن الهائلة وكشف إمكانية التجربة المتسامية.كما قال مارك روثكو مرة، "لم أصدق يوماً بأن هناك سؤال على الاطلاق عن التجريد والتمثيل. إنها فعلاً مسألة انهاء ذلك بالصمت والعزلة، وبالتنفس ومد الذراعين مرة أخرى". لوحات مان تقوم بالعمل ذاته. فرانكلين سيرمانز، أمين الفن المعاصر،متحف الفن كاونتي لوس أنجلوس.

Oculus, No.17, Oil on Canvas, 42"x54", 2019

Red Oculus, Oil on Canvas, 28"x34", 2019

Kasper de Gouw

His favorite subjects in bronze are animals. He reduced the forms almost to abstraction, as can be seen in birds, symbols for freedom. One work 7 birds wil be moving continuously al the time in the wind. This is mysterious and very special. There is a mythological aura in Kasper`s image which gives the feeling that they stem from prehistoric times. For more impressions visit my website.
www.kasperdegouw.nl or YouTube Kasper.de.gouw@planet.nl

مواضيعه المفضلة في البرونز هي الحيوانات. لقد قلل الأشكال وتوجه للتجريد تقريباً، كما يمكن ملاحظته في الطيور، رموز للحرية. ستتحرك 7 طيور بشكل مستمر في جميع الاوقات في مهب الريح. هذا غامض ومميز جداً. هناك هالة أسطورية في صورة كاسبر تعطي الشعور بأنها تنبع من عصور ما قبل التاريخ. لمزيد من الانطباعات قم بزيارة الموقع الإلكتروني.

7 Birds H 135 cm Bronze

Bird of paradise bronze H 20

Carolin Rechberg

Carolin Rechberg is an interdisciplinary Fine Artist born in Germany. She holds an Interdisciplinary BFA from the California College of the Arts, a MFA in Painting from the San Francisco Art Institute and an EdM in Art and Art Education from Teachers College, Columbia University. Rechberg has taught Drawing and Painting as a Teaching Assistant in her 1st Master at the San Francisco Art Institute, and Etching, Lithography, Silkscreen and Woodcut during her 2nd Master at Teachers College.

كارولين ريتشبيرغ فنانة فنون جميلة متعددة الاختصاصات ولدت في ألمانيا. حصلت على درجة بي اف اي في تعدد الاختصاصات من كلية الفنون في كاليفورنيا ، و ام اف اي في الرسم من معهد الفن في سان فرانسيسكو واي دي ام في الفن وتعليم الفن من كلية المعلمين، جامعة كولومبيا. درست ريتشبيرج الرسم والتلوين كمساعد مدرس في درجتها الماستر الأولى من معهد الفن في سان فرانسيسكو، والنقش، الطباعة الحجرية، والطباعة الحريرية، والنقش على الخشب أثناء درجتها الماستر الثانية في كلية المعلمين.

Origin, 213 x 269 cm. Painting: Mixed media on canvas

Witness, Mixed Media Painting on Canvas, 173x338cm

Barbara Krajewska

Barbara Krajewska was born in Poland but has lived in different countries. Profoundly European, she belongs to French culture that she represents with her books and other writings. Artist painter, she exhibited many times in Paris, but also in New York, in London, in Switzerland, in Italy and in Australia. She abandoned her initial technique, water painting, to work exclusively with oil on canvas. Barbara Krajewska is also an author. After completing her Ph.D. she published internationally four books and a number of articles devoted to French literature, French history, French society and also Napoleon and Dostoyevsky.

ولدت باربارا كرايوسكا في بولندا لكنها عاشت في بلدان أخرى. أصولها أوروبية، تنتمي للثقافة الفرنسية التي تقدمها في كتبها وكتاباتها الأخرى. فنانة رسامة، عرضت أعمالها مرات عدة في باريس، وفي نيويورك أيضاً، في لندن في سويسرا، في ايطاليا، وفي استراليا. هجرت طريقتها الأولية، الرسم المائي، لتعمل حصرياً في اللوحات الزيتيو. تعمل باربارا كرايوسكا كمؤلفة. بعد انهاء درجة الدكتوراه نشرت أربعة كتب عالمياً وعدداً من المقالات مكرسة للأدب الفرنسي، التاريخ الفرنسي، المجتمع الفرنسي، وأيضاً نابليون ودوستويفسكي.

Nu couché en mauve (nude in mauve)

Mère et fils (mother and her son)

Howard Harris

American-born photographer Howard Harris, in his carefully altered digital prints, takes on what is perhaps the most American of themes: the interrelationship of perception and technology. Harris explores how the whole emotional complex underlying one's personality integrates into the structural logic of architecture and design. As Harris himself frames it, "my aim to combine technology and aesthetics in a way that expands the viewer's experience of photographic art. Because, visual reality is an ever-shifting, highly individualized experience. In any given moment, what we see reflects both our inner state and a synthesis of outer qualities—light, color, movement, space. My exploration in dimensional photographic art represents an attempt to recreate the perceptual experience, with its dynamic nature and hidden complexities. In my patented process I use photographic constructions, a single often abstracted image is layered over itself on clear acrylic surfaces and superimposed on a subtle grid. The resulting visual phenomenon infuses the image with a sense of dimensionality and fluidity affected by such changes as the angle of viewing and light. However, perceptual mechanics are only part of the equation. Equally essential are universal principles of design that produce qualities we perceive as beauty.

هوارد هاريس مصور فوتوغرافي من مواليد أمريكا، في مطبوعاته الرقمية المغيرة بعناية، يتناول على الأرجح أكثر المواضيع الأمريكية: الترابط بين الإدراك والتكنولوجيا. استكشف هاريس كيف يندمج المركب العاطفي برمته الذي يكمن وراء شخصية الفرد داخل المنطق الهيكلي للعمارة والتصميم. كما عبر عنها هاريس نفسه، "أهدف للجمع بين التكنولوجيا والجماليات بطريقة توسع خبرة المشاهد في فن التصوير الفوتوغرافي.وذلك لأن، الواقع الافتراضي شكل طفرة غير مسبوقة، تجربة فردية للغاية. في أي لحظة، ما نراه يعكس كلا من حالتنا الداخلية وتوليفة من الصفات الخارجية __ الضوء، اللون، الحركة، الفضاء. استكشافي في فن التصوير الفوتوغرافي البعدي يقدم محاولة لاعادة صنع الخبرة الادراكية، بطبيعتها الديناميكية وتعقيداتها المخفية. في طريقة معالجتي الحائزة على براءة اختراع أستخدم البناء الفوتوغرافي، غالبًا ما يتم وضع صورة مفردة يتم تجريدها فوق نفسها على أسطح أكريليك شفافة ويتم تركيبها على شبكة دقيقة. تضفي الظاهرة المرئية الناتجة على الصورة إحساسًا بالأبعاد والتدفق متأثرة بمتغيرات كزاوية الرؤية والضوء. لكن، ميكانيكا الادراك جزء من المعادلة فقط. بنفس القدر من الأهمية ، هناك مبادئ كونية للتصميم تنتج صفات نعتبرها جمالًا.

Patterns

Hospitality

Michal Ashkenasi

My work is about feelings, my mood when I make it, the situation of my country, my surroundings, the world and people. I work from my imagination from a dream or an association from something. My art has different structures, big fields of colour with a small object. Most of my work is minimalistic-abstract. I came very late to art, only when I was 43 years old. I never thought to become an artist but I'm happy it became so. For me, it is the only way to show my true self and am glad to share it with other people!

عملي كله حول المشاعر، مزاجي عندما أقوم به، موقف بلدي، ما يحيط بي، العالم والناس. أعمل منطلقاً من خيالي أو من حلم أو من ارتباط بشيء ما. يمتلك فني هياكل مختلفة، نطاقات ألوان واسعة مع موضوع صغير. معظم أعمالي ضيقة الحدود ملخصة. أتيت للفن متأخراً جداً. عندما وصل عمري 43 عاماً. لم أفكر يوماً بأن أكون فناناً لكنني سعيد بكوني كذلك. بالنسبة لي هي الطريقة الوحيدة لأظهر نفسي على حقيقتها وأنا ممتن لأشارك ذلك مع الآخرين.

Two Lakes, One Point

Flowers

Jasmine Seo

United States | الولايات المتحدة الأمريكية

My name is Jasmine and I am a surrealist with a propensity for enlightenment and an optimistic approach to life. Although I mostly work with pastels, I have been particularly enjoying incorporating illustration and printmaking techniques in my artwork as a powerful communication tool to help our society broaden their sense of understanding and wisdom for better harmony and peace, not only within ourselves but also in our life. In my artwork, personified animals are embodied in the process of re-discovering a ray of hope that might have faded and been lost in the pandemonium during our individual lifelong journey. The perspectives through my inner child's eye are intended to bring every one of us together to the point where we can reflect upon the past and present, and work towards a better future together.

اسمي ياسمين وأنا سريالية أميل للتنوير ونهجي متفائل في الحياة. على الرغم من أنني أعمل في الغالب مع الباستيل ، إلا أنني كنت أستمتع بشكل خاص بدمج تقنيات الرسم التوضيحي والطباعة في أعمالي الفنية كأداة اتصال قوية لمساعدة مجتمعنا على توسيع إحساسهم بالفهم والحكمة من أجل انسجام وسلام أفضل، ليس داخل أنفسنا فقط وإنما في حياتنا أيضاً. في أعمالي الفنية ، تتجسد الحيوانات المجسدة في عملية إعادة اكتشاف شعاع الأمل الذي ربما يكون قد تلاشى وفقد خلال صخب رحلتنا الفردية على مر حياتنا. تهدف وجهات النظر من خلال عين الطفل الذي يكمن داخلي إلى جلب كل منا معاً إلى النقطة التي تمكننا من التفكير في الماضي والحاضر ، والعمل معًا نحو مستقبل أفضل.

Le Penseur (The Thinker)

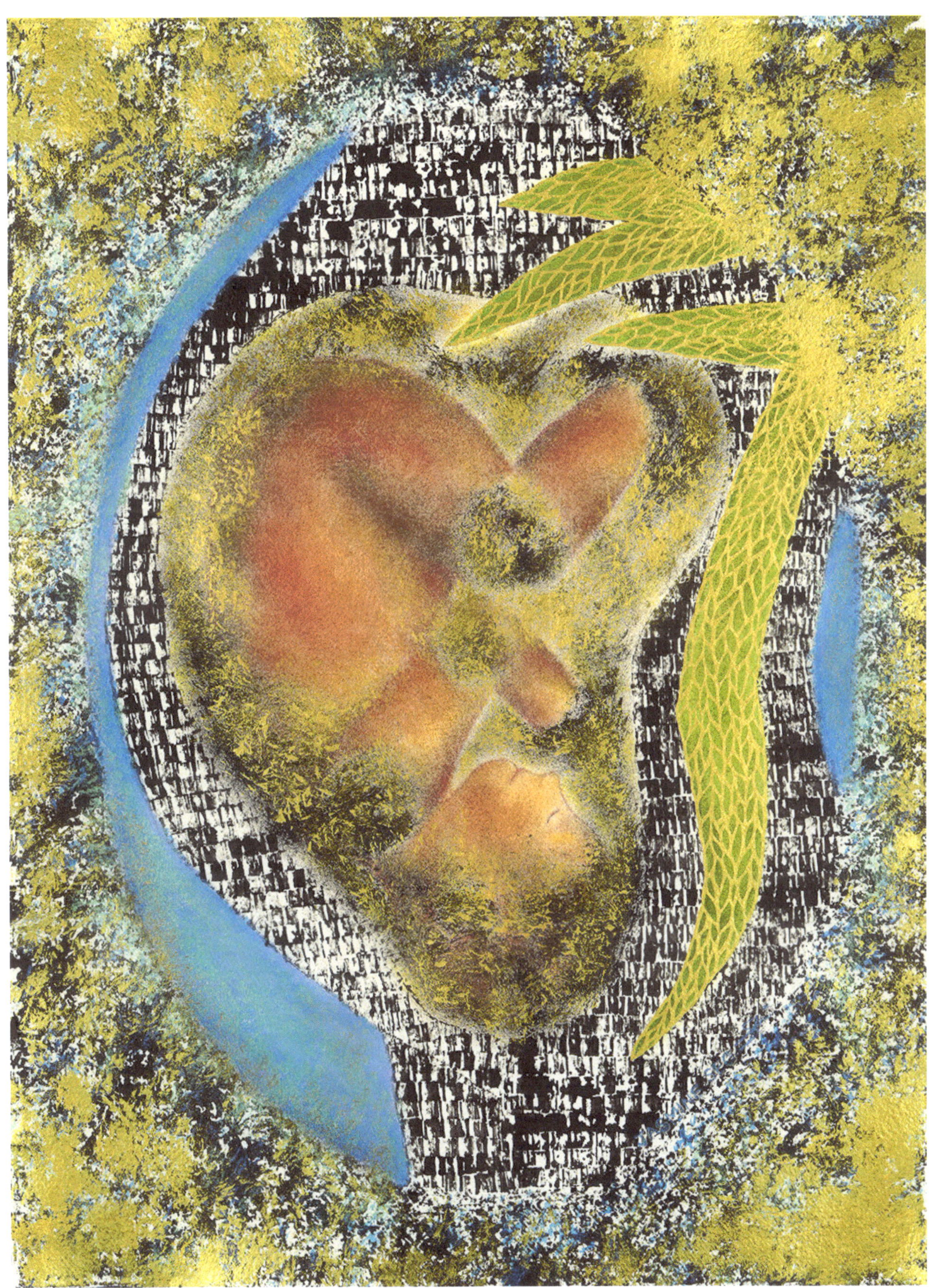

9E:6irth (RE:birth)

David Turner FRSA,"More Strange then True", 2018.

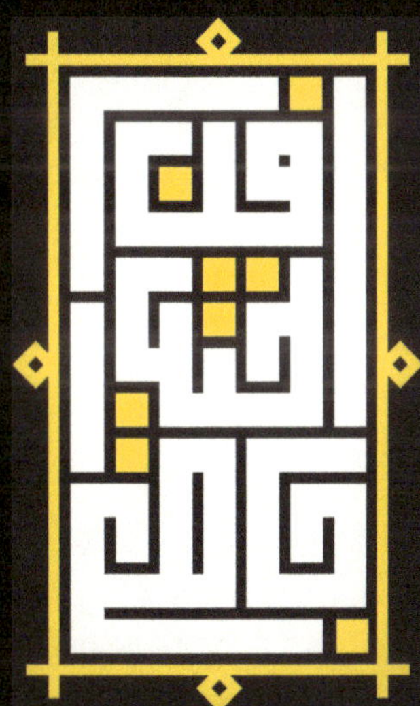

Published by
**Contemporary
Art Station**

كونتيمبوراري أرت ستيشن/ أي سي ام جيستورا كلتشرال، اس ال
جميع الأعمال الفنية @ 2021 أعمال الفنانين الفردية.
القياسات والعناوين للأعمال الفنية زودت من قبل الفنانين.

First published in April 2021 by the
Contemporary Art Station / ICM Gestora Cultural, SL
All artworks @ 2021 the individual artists.
Measurements and titles of artworks are supplied by the artists.

أول نشر في المملكة المتحدة تاريخ مارس 2021 بواسطة
كونتيمبوراري أرت ستيشن/ أي سي ام جيستورا كلتشرال، اس ال
جميع الأعمال الفنية @ 2021 أعمال الفنانين الفردية.
القياسات والعناوين للأعمال الفنية زودت من قبل الفنانين.